MW01702175

Maximizing Your Expectations
Q & A EDITION
Butler's Guide

Kenton A. Grayson

MAXIMIZING YOUR EXPECTATION.
Copyright © 2022. Kenton A. Grayson. All Rights Reserved.

Printed in the United States of America.

No portion of this book may be reproduced, stored in a retrieval system, or transmitted in any form or by any means, except for brief quotations in printed reviews, without the prior written permission of DayeLight Publishers or Kenton A. Grayson.

Published by

DAYELight PUBLISHERS

ISBN: 978-1-958443-01-9 (paperback)

Most frequently asked questions regarding butler service in the hospitality industry or a customer's guideline to butler service, i.e., through questions and answers.

Dedication

I dedicate this book to the billions of tourists who travel around the world. A few are at a crossroads trying to decide whether they should book butler service or not.

For guest who would like to experience the service but are afraid to ask for anything and for couples or families who pay thousands of dollars but does not know what to expect from butlers. I dedicate my efforts in shedding some light on your vacation by answering some of the most frequently asked questions regarding having a butler.

Due to butler service now being the fastest growing business in the hotel industry, whereas most hotels are expanding on the number of rooms and accommodations, this significant and rapid change allows stakeholders to increase their investment by asking for three times more just by adding a butler (personal assistant) to the accommodation packages.

I am here to dedicate and share my knowledge with anyone who decides to take on the role of a butler or anyone who wishes to experience the service of a butler.

Disclaimer:

If you purchased this book without a cover, you should be aware that this book is stolen property. It was reported as "Unsold and destroyed" to the publisher, and neither the author nor the publisher has received any payment for this "Stripped" book.

Acknowledgments

I just want to say a big thank you to my wife, Tiffany B. Grayson, for staying with me and also for journeying with me through those sleepless nights.

Thanks to my mother, Gloria B. Forrester, for moral, motivational, and spiritual support.

A big thank you to my one and only sister, Moesha Forrester, and my five brothers, Leon Nelson, Gart Bowen, Calvin Foster, Damion Witter, and Kourtney Grayson, who encouraged me to never give up throughout my rough time in writing this book.

Table of Content

QUESTIONS
&
ANSWERS

Please allow me to start off my book by saying: No butler is bigger than a guest COMPLAINING on them, and no COMPLAINT is bigger than the butler because we are problem-solvers.

WHO IS A BUTLER?

The dictionary defines a butler as:

- The chief male servant of a household who is in charge of other employees, receives guests, directs the serving of meals, and performs various personal services.

- A manservant having charge of the wines and liquors.

A butler is an elite-trained staff who specializes in delivering the highest standard of guest expectation. They are service professionals who are knowledgeable and understands all the areas of operations within the hotel & villa. These staff take pride in providing the highest level of service to their guest. The butler can be referred to as a one-stop shop for all information and request.

For many persons, when they think of a butler, the first thing that comes to mind is the television show "Fresh Prince of Bel-Air." In the hotel, the service is a little different but maintains that personal assistant concept. See below for a few **characteristics** that a butler must display:

a) Must be honest and trustworthy.
b) Must be properly groomed at all times.
c) Must have patience.
d) Must be a good team player.
e) Must be a good listener and problem solver.
f) Must be knowledgeable about his/her products and the culture in which he/she operates and live in.
g) Must know how to anticipate and exceed guest expectations without intruding on their privacy.

Just to name and list a few.

WHEN AND WHERE DID BUTLER SERVICE START?

The modern butler began around the early **1920s** (following World War I). Employment in domestic service occupations began a sharp overall decline in western European countries and even more remarkably in the United States. The word "butler" comes from Anglo-Norman "buteler" which is a variant. Old Norman *Butelier, derived of boteille "bottle." The premise of which the butler (or the bottle) is the role associated with the chief member of staff in the household, the staff member entrusted with the care and serving of the wine. Although certain wines are still highly valuable, in the old days, the wine cellar of the wealthy would have held considerable value and thus would have only been entrusted to the most senior of staff in the household.

Interestingly, in Britain where the butler seems to have become the most commonplace for this type of staff member to exist, they were originally a middle-ranking member of staff of a wealthy household. By the 17th and 18th centuries, the role of the butler developed into a more senior position, normally held by a man, and was seen as the highest position of staff within the grand household.

Households would require the butler to wear a special uniform to separate him from the junior servants, which in the modern butler is seen as the morning suit. Today, however, the modern butler is most likely to be dressed in a business suit or dress according to the principal's request, be it informal or a formally run household.

The phrase "silver service" or "silver butler" developed in line with the butler having expertise and professional knowledge of management, inventory, storage, use, and cleaning of the silverware in the house, including all the associated tableware and service in line with silver service.

Throughout the ages, the butler has been present in history and literature and was often used as a gauge to assess the wealth of a family. Less wealthy families may have a maid or nanny, but the wealthiest families had at least one butler. The largest properties would have a multitude of servants, from footmen, maids, scullery maids, nannies, lady's maids, coachmen, groom(s), and the head of the staff, the butler.

The staff in the house would follow a set hierarchy within the household, and only the butler (and the under-butler, if there was one) would be called by their first names. All other servants would be called "Mr. [surname]." By calling the butler by his first name, it suggests that the role of the butler transcends the typical "place" of the servant and suggests that the butler straddles both servant and member of the family. This informal approach is extremely revealing as to the wealthy family's view of the butler himself.

Regardless of this straddle between the two sides, the butler was not afraid to get stuck in any difficult position and would at a moment's notice assist other servants should he be required to. His main focus was to ensure that the household ran smoothly and the principals' needs were taken care of.

Although historically in Britain, you were typically born into becoming a servant, you still retained human rights and were paid for the work you did. Therefore, the role of the butler was coveted as it gave not only responsibility and social standing both in and outside of the home, but it also provided the highest income within the servant hierarchy.

In America, from a historical perspective, the role of servants was typically found in the slave trade, and particularly affluent homes would ensure that a male slave was refined and placed as the butler of the home. They were not paid for their service, and the life of a black slave, even in the role of the butler, could be heinous depending on the type of master who owned them.

Starting in the 1920s, Britain saw a dramatic decline in domestic service and by the mid-1980s domestic service was at an all-time low. It is usual that as the social classes within a culture align themselves, the "upstairs/downstairs" mentality falls away, and the concept of domestic service becomes an ungainly past-time.

In the last decade, however, the role of the butler has seen a dramatic increase, with both wealthy families wanting to hire a butler and individuals wishing to be hired. It is no longer seen as a servitude, but a choice. As with fine dining, 5-star hotels, and luxury lifestyle, the butler has become a symbol of wealth and success, and principals around the world have realized the importance of hiring a butler in their homes.

The modern butler may be a symbol, but in reality, they are much, much more than that. They can be a cultural connection between the principal and the country, with butlers often advising their principal on the best place to buy suits or cigars. They will often have a business-like mind and be able to run the properties and affairs of the clients with precision and care. Butlers are often in charge of recruiting new staff, managing affairs, and ensuring that the household is run to the highest level and standard expected.

Modern butlers prepare the house to ensure that the principal arrives to find the property exactly how they expect it to appear. They ensure the finishing touches are executed with precision, and every event and dinner party that is held in the home is run without a hitch. Today, men and women of all backgrounds are seeking new employment opportunities, and the thought of service is no longer a dirty word. In fact, the art of service is something that the very highest caliber of butlers pride themselves on.

In modern literature and film, we have seen a rise of the butler. From Batman through to Downtown Abby, the role of the butler is one that both intrigues and fascinates people, and rightly so, the most important aspect of being a butler is discretion, and "What the butler saw" is indeed a subject that entertains and delights. A high-quality butler will never reveal details of what they saw, but even the suggestions of what they have born witness to is a highly fascinating subject worthy of many great books of literature to come.

WHAT IS THE ROLE OF A BUTLER?

A butler is like a button that holds the family together. His many duties and responsibilities can take the weight off a busy family, particularly when that family has many tasks at hand and perhaps when both adults work long hours. A butler can also be for those who can afford it and who would like to spend that extra time on leisure and hobbies, entrusting homely affairs to an individual they feel they can count on.

The butler's job is to meet the guest's preferences such as the guest's likes and dislikes, and also for the guest to have an enjoyable and memorable vacation.

The butler's job is:

- To anticipate customers' needs and wants.
- Cleaning and maintenance.
- Care for clothing.
- Care for fine china, silver, crystal (villa butler).
- Care for an inventory of artwork and antiques (villa butler).
- Security of their employer and residence.
- Coordination and scheduling of service contractors.
- To ensure that their guest has a relaxed, enjoyable, and memorable stay at the resort.
- To surpass customers' expectations.
- To ensure that all your request is met in a timely manner.
- To ensure your surroundings are clean and tidy at all times.
- If there are any allergies, to ensure that the different food outlets are fully aware of the allergies that the guest has.

This list is not exhaustive as there are much more responsibilities, all based on the job.

WHAT SHOULD I ASK MY BUTLER TO DO FOR ME?

Good butlers do more than simply run errands; they anticipate the needs of their guests and possess the flexibility and social grace for interaction with people of all ages and cultures. They are affable, knowledgeable, impeccably groomed, and, of course, discreet. Still, sometimes even the most well-meaning client crosses the line when it comes to their butler requests. To keep this from happening to you, I always say you can ask your butler for every and anything; no request is too weird to ask the butler for once it is legal and ethical.

Here are a few things you can ask for:

- You can ask your butler to reserve a chair on the pool or beach.
- You can ask your butler to unpack your suitcase.
- You can ask your butler to book tours, spa, dinner reservations on and off the resort/villa, golf, and watersport activity.
- You can ask your butler to book entertainment activities such as tennis, volleyball, or game shows with your entertainment team.

- You can ask your butler to book a romantic setting such as candlelight dining in the room, on the pool deck, on the beach under the stars, perhaps a garden setting while you dine. You can listen to outdoor nature at its best or draw a warm romantic rose petal bubble bath and transform your bedroom into a fairytale romantic towel fold land.
- You can ask your butler to assist with laundry services as well as ensure your room is clean (lining and towel), and the minibar is replenished while you are out of the room.

WHY DO I NEED A BUTLER?

The reason why I strongly recommend butler service is because guests without butler service would have to do everything on their own, which would take away from their vacation time, like standing in line to book events, dinners, spa, tours, or running back and forth trying to find their travel agent to figure out their transportation back to the airport or their flight details, just to name a few. While a guest with a butler would spend more time on the beach, pool, or at dinner, if there is anything they need, their personal assistant would be just a phone call away. Rest assured that he/she will take care of your request while you enjoy your vacation to the fullest.

WHAT SHOULD I EXPECT FROM MY BUTLER?

The first thing I would say is to expect your butler to ask a lot of questions within the first twenty minutes of your arrival in order for he/she to have a better understanding or to be better familiar with your needs. This will give him/her an opportunity on how to personalize or tailor the service they offer to your requirements. Your butler is expected to be very professional, fun, and interactive.

I want to expound on a few things you should expect from your butler:

Meet and Greet

The butler is often the first point of contact in the household and hotel industry, whether this is over the phone, at the front door or gate, and when welcoming guests. The butler can welcome you or any visitor in the correct manner, take your coat and bags, and in case of parties or events, guide your guests to the right location on the property.

Food and Drink Service

Expect your professional butler to be trained and specialize in silver service. Your butler can set your table in any way required. This might be a simple weekday meal, where the butler can make sure the table is set and serve the food, or it may be a formal dinner party where the butler can provide full professional table settings.

HOUSEKEEPING/LAUNDRY

Expect your butlers to be experts in cleaning and laundry services. They can either assist already present housekeepers, manage the housekeeper and check or correct their work, or be fully responsible for the housekeeping in the house. When making a butler fully responsible for all the housekeeping and laundry, set realistic expectations.

A butler can be in charge of household staff, managing routes, organizing payments, and arranging events when needed.

NOTE: For Villa
They can also be in charge of recruiting new members of staff, disciplining staff where needed, and providing training and guidance.

Personal Assistant/Confidant

Expect your male or female butlers to be perfect personal aides or confidants. They are excellent in assessing situations, and will know you and the way you like your life to look through and through. Butlers will hold the highest level of discretion and will never give away any information. They can be there for you after a long, stressful day, to give advice, or just to lend a listening ear.

WHAT IS A GOOD BOTTLE OF WINE TO DRINK?

Most customers who book butler service enjoy wine; this question is one that is asked close to dinner time or at dinner. A great bottle of wine often depends on three main factors:

1. The meal the wine is paired with.
2. The temperature of the storage and serving of the wine.
3. Selecting the right wine.

The pairing of wine is where most new lover of wine make their mistake because they love a particular wine, whether it is red or white. They try to have that wine with every and anything they are having but, news flash, both wines don't pair with any and any food. There is a table below to show the different meals or meats that red, white, and blush wine pair with. If you are a lover of seafood and love red wine, then you are in for trouble as the content of the red wine doesn't compliment the seafood. Seafood dish is often consumed and paired well with white wine.

Varietals	Seafood	Poultry	Meat	Cheese	Herbs
Cabernet Sauvignon	Tuna, Salmon	Quail, Duck Squab	Beef, Lamb, Venison	Aged Cheddar, Parmesan, Provolone, Aged Gouda	Thyme, rosemary, Bay Leaf, Parsley
Chardonnay	Salmon, Tuna,	Chicken, Turkey,	Pork, Veal	Jarlsberg, Brie, Camembert, Munster	Tarragon, Chervil, Dill, Italian Parsley
Gewurztraminer	Scallops, Crab, Smoked Salmon	Turkey, Chicken	Pork, Ham, Prosciutto	Smoked Gouda, Goat Cheese, Gorgonzola	Ginger, Curry, Cilantro
Gruner Veltliner	Halibut, Sole, Sea Bass	Turkey, Chicken, Game Hen	Pork, Veal	Brie, Gouda, Feta	Coriander, Caraway, Dill
Merlot	Salmon, Tuna,	Quail, Duck, Squab	Beef, Lamb, Venison	Aged Cheddar, Parmesan, Provolone, Aged Gouda	Basil, Thyme, Mint, Italian Parsley
Petite Sirah	Salmon, Tuna,	Chicken, Game Hen, Duck, Quail	Beef, Lamb, Italian Sausage	Asiago, Aged Goat Cheese, Cheddar	Thyme, Basil, Bay Leaf, Italian Parsley
Pinot Grigio	Trout, Crab, Swordfish,	Chicken, Turkey, Game Hen	Pork, Prosciutto	Ricotta, Fontina, Provolone	Basil, Chervil, Italian Parsley
Pinot Noir	Salmon, Tuna, Swordfish	Quail, Duck, Squab	Lamb, Pork, Italian Sausage, Boar	Parmesan, Asiago, Fontina, Cambozola	Thyme, Fennel, Basil, Italian Parsley
Primitivo	Cioppino, Tuna, Bouillabaisse	Quail, Duck, Game Hens	Lamb, Beef, Italian Sausage	Parmesan, Asiago, Fontina, Ricotta Salata	Basil, Oregano, Thyme, Italian Parsley
Rose	Salmon, Shellfish, Grilled Sea Bass, Trout	Chicken, Chicken Apple Sausage, Game Hen	Pork, Ham, Prosciutto	Goat Cheese, Parmesan, Feta, Gouda, Munster	Italian Parsley, Basil, Chervil, Chives, Curry
Sangiovese	Tuna, Swordfish	Duck, Quail, Squab	Lamb, Pork, Beef	Asiago, Fontina, Parmesan, Ricotta	Basil, Thyme, Bay Leaf, Fennell
Sauvignon Blanc	Oyster, Crab, Sole, Trout	Chicken, Turkey, Game Hens	Pork, Veal	Goat Cheese, Feta, Gorgonzola, Ricotta, Fresh Mozzarella	Dill, Chervil, Chives, Parsley
Zinfandel	Tuna, Cioppino, Bouillabaisse	Duck, Quail, Pheasant, Chicken	Beef, Lamb, Barbecue Ribs, Italian Sausage	Asiago, Gouda, Parmesan, Dry Jack, Aged Gouda	Black Pepper, Basil, Thyme, Fennel, Parsley

When pairing bottles of wine or champagnes, these factors should be taken into consideration:

- how sugary the wine is.
- how much acid the wine contains.
- how fruity the wine is.
- how tannins the wine is.
- how much alcohol the wine contains.

The reason why you would have to take these factors in mind is because there are certain elements of food that complement wines. The elements of food to consider are how much fat the food contains, how acidic the food that you are consuming is, how salty the meal is, how sweet the meals are, how bitter the meal is, and the texture of the meal.

When we think about pairing, we think about how these flavor elements are going to work together.

Note:
A big factor that most people often overlook is where and at what temperature the wine is stored. For persons who live in the Caribbean where the temperature of the sun is much hotter than in the USA, Canada, or the United Kingdom, just to name a few places, it is recommended that you put the red wine in a cooler to keep the wine at a temperature of 60 degrees F which is 15,5°C.

Selecting the right wine for a meal can be very hard but let us break it down a bit:

a) When having hors d'oeuvres, you would pair it with a dry rose, which is very flavorful, and usually hoes d'oeuvres contain many different flavors.
b) "Acidic need acidic." Any food/meal that has a high acidic flavor that you would normally squeeze lemon or infuse with lemon flavor would go well with a light acidic white wine like pinot grigio or savion blank.
c) Tanning needs fat; meals like rabbi steak or brazed duck would require a bold or full body red wine such as cabernet or Syrah to balance out the fat in the meal.
d) Heat needs sweat. If you are having a dish with a little spice or a lot of spice, you are going to need a lightly sweet wine to pair with it, such as riesling or a white zinfandel.
e) Salty needs bubbles. It is very hard to pair salty food with wine unless it is a bubbly drink such as champagne. The carbonation of the Sparkling Wine has a whole new flavor and adds a new texture to the meal.
f) Earthy needs earthy, for example, mushroom and lintel, which is a gaming meat (an animal

that you often hunt). These pair well with syrah are a pinot noir.

When pairing your wine, these above factors are what you need to take into consideration for your wine to compliment the meal to the fullest.

CAN THE BUTLER HAVE SEXUAL INTERCOURSE WITH A GUEST?

No!

However, we do have cases where this happens. Sometimes people find love in unexpected places.

We have heard of cases where the husband pays the butler to have sex with his wife. Now the price to do so is usually high, more than what they normally tip the butler or butlers.

If a butler finds him/herself in a situation like this, I recommend that he/she reports the situation to the manager in charge. If the butler is not interested, it becomes very uncomfortable working with these guests. The butler has the right to decline taking care of these guests. At that point, the manager would decide on how the situation is handled. The butler has the right to request a change team or time off from work until these guests check out or reserve the right to file a police report. The general manager also has the right to ask the guest to leave the resort.

CAN THE BUTLER BUY DRUGS FOR A GUEST?

No!

Note:
There is a promise that we will do whatever is legal and ethical to make our guests happy.

Once it is illegal, the butler will explain that such services are not something that can be carried out by him/her due to the policy of the hotel, and it is something that he/she can be charged with in court. Some clients can be a bit demanding, and once they are told that the butler will not be able to carry out such a request, they might be upset, and, in most cases, the guest requests a change of team and refer to their butler as being incompetent. In cases like this, the butler would explain the situation to his/her manager, who will speak with the customer in the presence of security, and the aim is to explain and enforce the policy of the hotel; no team member should be promoting or distributing any form of drugs to guest. Butlers are usually trained on how to deal with situations such as this in a professional manner.

WHAT IS A GOOD TIP FOR A BUTLER?

This is a frequently asked question mostly by first-timers and, most time, at the beginning of their vacation. A butler's response is usually "Based on the level of service you receive, you can use your discretion. You can tip accordingly."

What if you think your butler went above and beyond throughout your vacation, US$150 per butler upwards.

If you think you have received nothing special and they didn't do much in terms of service to "wow" you throughout your vacation, then anywhere between US$0-50.

Note:
In some cases, butlers have observed guests who believe they have given their butler a very great tip, and this may be the best tip they have ever received; at that moment, the amount turns out to be average.

I recommend that you tip your butler according to the service you have received. We have seen where the butler delivers an exceptional service to their guest and, in the end, the guest gave them up to US$10,000 for a tip, purchase a house or pay for a car or even book a flight for their butler to vacation with them, just to name a few things. Butlers often receive gifts as a good gesture for their outstanding performance as mentioned above. Tip according to the service you received.

WHAT'S THE MOST POPULAR REQUEST A GUEST HAS ASKED A BUTLER FOR?

One of the most popular requests a guest has asked their butler for is asking for drugs and sex; some of them tend to be very adamant about it throughout their stay. Please note that this is something that is illegal that will lead up to the butler losing his or her job. If the butler is not into contrabands, then he or she becomes very uncomfortable around and with their guest.

On the other hand, you will find butler/s who find pleasure in selling drugs. They view this as a form of fast money that he/she doesn't have to work for. This requires putting their jobs on the line, which would not put their minds at ease because the guest purchased the drugs. The butler would not be sure if they are a secret shopper or spy hired by the hotel to see who is breaking the rules.

Please note:
We do have cases where the hotel employs person/s to travel on vacation and pose as a guest to audit the persons who are not working with the standard or working illegally in the hotel. At times, these customers

are expected to ask for everything that is bad or not a part of the standard. They are expected to complete a report of their experience and, most times, names do come on that report or even pictures, and some persons lose their jobs. Managers must document or suspend, and the list goes on. I would recommend sticking with the standard of the hotel and doing whatever is legal and ethical to accommodate your guest and not cost you your job.

HAVE YOU EVER BUTLER ANYONE FAMOUS?

Oh yes, all the time. Because of our job profile, butlers always have the first preference to care for V.I.Ps., for example, prime ministers, general managers, or top managers from different companies. All guests are very important to the butler.

Just to name a few:

- Bob Marley family and company.
- Daymond Johns; he is the owner of the clothing line FUBU.

There were a lot more, such as a prince from Nigeria, Prime Ministers across the Caribbean, CEO for mega companies across the world; because of their status, there is a high level of confidence. If you get my next book, I might tell you some of their secrets.

HOW LONG HAVE YOU BEEN A BUTLER?

I have been a butler since 2010 but have been in the service industry since 2007. I have worked at five different resorts, including one villa, and I am still employed in a leading hotel on the island of Jamaica, where I am still able to shine and leave a mark on so many lives around the world in so many different ways—one day at a time and one guest at a time.

DID YOU HAVE TO GO TO SCHOOL FOR BUTLER SERVICE?

Yes, I did. Given the high demand for butlers in hotels, villas, and homes, there are so many institutions today around the world that offer training.

The ones that are more recognized are the ones that are in the UK and Thailand.

I am trained by the Guild of Professional English Butler, where I received a distinction. I also did another training with Exceeding Customer's Expectations which is endorsed by the University of England and the Federation of International Business Academy USA (FIB).

It is safe to say I do understand the English way of butler service; however, the Caribbean put a little bit of changes to give it a more laid-back vibes, which allows the customer to feel more at home and more open to asking questions.

Some customers prefer not to call you a butler but friend or by your name. Their remarks are: it makes them feel and sound like we are their slave or helper. For most butlers like myself, and some of my colleagues, we are honored to be called butlers.

WHAT IS THE DURATION OF THE BUTLER TRAINING?

Butler training never STOPS! Yes! NEVER STOPS!

This job deals with people's needs and wants. Every day you learn something new about your guest and their culture, but on the other hand, some institution's class training last for two weeks or even up to six months.

For most hotels, what they do when you are a new butler is they would place you to work with someone who is more senior, meaning that person has more experience than you to guide you on your development path. Most times, you will be tested on your knowledge to see how well you are grasping the information as well as how well you are applying the knowledge to your day-to-day job.

I have been in butler service for over ten years, and I am still learning new things and ways to deal with guests' problems. The hospitality industry is not one of those jobs that you can say you have mastered. What you can say is that you are very good at it, but you can never master people's needs and wants as this changes ever so often and according to their mood as well.

WHAT IS YOUR MOST EMBARRASSING MOMENT BEING A BUTLER?

Every butler faces some level of embarrassment during their careers. The most embarrassing moment I can remember was when I was training to become a butler. I was an engineer before I became a butler. I had no experience in the food and beverage department. The approach I took was to go to the restaurant to learn how to set and clear tables. One day I said, "Yes, I am ready to serve a table by myself. Yes! I AM READY." I got a candlelight dinner on the beach. They were newlyweds, and they paid for this dinner. I got my first two guests seated. I seated them fine, I introduced myself well, took their orders, and offered water and wine. I poured the water perfectly, but while I was pouring the red wine into a glass for the guest, the wind blew the wine all over the white tablecloth because my hand was too high up from the glass. While the guests were having their romantic candlelight dinner, it was all messed up. I had to change the tablecloth in the middle of the dinner. However, it was very windy as it was on the beach. Of course, I had to apologize to the guests, but they understood, and we all made jokes about it after.

Throughout the meal, the guests ended up tipping me after, and I was the first and only butler on training over those two weeks to receive a tip while on training.

CAN THE BUTLER HAVE A DRINK OF ALCOHOL WITH A GUEST?

No!

It is not recommended that staff do so because not every person can drink and maintain a high level of professionalism while on the job. On the other hand, we do have cases where butlers have a drink with their guests because some guests find it offensive when they keep on asking, and the butler keeps on saying no.

Let me share an experience I had with a German guest. He was staying at the hotel where I was working for two weeks. He got so comfortable with me as his butler to the point that he saw me as family. I understood why he felt that way. I knew all his preferences. In the first three days, I understood his movements and operations, such as time for vodka, time for cigar, even his wife's vodka martinis, and before he could even think about lunch, I was right there. He kept on asking me to sit and have a drink with him. I kept on saying no; kept on saying no. One day he offered me a glass of cranberry and vodka, and I said no, and he got very upset with me because I didn't want to drink with him. I was trying to maintain my professionalism, but this couple didn't care about my professionalism; they thought it was like having a drink with a close friend—a new extension of their family—that they met on vacation. Of course, it led to the point where he met my manager at the time and expressed his concern and, yes, after that we did drink for the remainder of their stay.

CAN THE BUTLER HAVE DINNER WITH HIS/HER GUESTS?

Yes and no. It all goes back to the resort/villa that you are working for. Some resorts do allow their butler to dine with their guests while others don't. The ones that don't are really trying to protect the butler's reputation with the guests as alcohol is often involved in dining, and they don't want the butler to get drunk. Some butlers dine with the guests and feel as if they are equal and lose focus and professionalism while they are taking care of the guests. They often feel as if they and the guests are friends. We do have cases where the hotel/villa doesn't allow staff to eat with guests, but the guests keep on pursuing/requesting the matter for many reasons, for example, that guest can be a multi-time return guest to the resort and keep on requesting the same butler to take care of them. The hotel will not deny the guest's request but grant their request. Remember, a good villa or hotel should be all about guest satisfaction.

HOW DO I KNOW I HAVE A GOOD BUTLER?

Within the first five minutes of meeting your butler, you will know if he or she will be a great butler. Remember that your personality also has a lot to do with how the butler behaves around you. Within the first day, you can know if the butler is all about the money and not looking out for you having a wonderful time. If you come on vacation to have FUN, UNWINE, and experience a new culture, if you are open and willing to trust them, then you can get the best out of your butler.

Please note:
The butler can meet you not on his/her "A" game when really and truly the butler just needed a few minutes to get his/her act together. I always say that whenever a guest goes on vacation, they need 24-hours to get in the mood for their vacation. The reason is that they often

suffer from jet lag, airport drama, and even the drive from the airport can be a bit of a mood changer, but it is nothing that a little sleep or a nice drink from the bar can't fix.

CAN A BUTLER GO OFF THE RESORT WITH A GUEST?

Yes and no. It all depends on the resort policy and where the guest would want the butler to accompany them to.

Most times on a resort, the butler doesn't usually take care of only one family or one guest, so if the butler leaves the resort to accompany one guest/family off the resort and leave other guests at the resort, then the butler would be abandoning their job/other guests.

There are protocols that the butler must follow. Even if the butler is off duty, the butler would have to reach out to his or her leader for permission for this to be done, and if the butler decides to take it up on his/herself to engage such activities, it will result in the loss of their job if anything should happen while they are out with the guest.

One of the main reasons for this is, whenever the guest leaves the resort, the hotel has no control over their health and safety, so hotels are very cautious pertaining to this matter, but the fact is, if the butler is there, it now becomes the hotel's problem as well.

The butler is an ambassador for the hotel, and as an ambassador of the hotel/villa, the butler should never lose focus and never drop the resort standard on and off the resort.

In the event of the hotel giving the butler permission to leave the resort, please allow me to list a few places that the butler might be permitted to accompany the guests to:

- Night Clubs
- Excursions
- Have dinner off the resort upon the guest's request.
- Shopping
- Sightseeing around the nearby town.
- To the airport to welcome you or to say farewell depending on the level of relationship that the guests have with the butler.
- If you must go to the hospital depending on the butler/hotel.

Just to name a few.

CAN THE BUTLER GO PARTYING WITH THEIR GUESTS?

Yes, at the butler's own discretion, depending on the butler's religious beliefs. However, some resorts do not support this practice as the employer cannot control the amount of alcohol the butler is consuming. Therefore, this may result in the butler not being professional during the time they are partying.

If the guest has a complaint about any incident that took place at the party, it will result in the butler being terminated from the company without any further questions.

In most cases, the guest would ask their butler to recommend the best place to party on the island near the resort. The butler will make his/her suggestion. The question that always follows is, "Will I see you there?" or "Can you accompany us there?" This is often because the guest feels comfortable around their butler and the butler's presence at the location makes them feel safe. Whenever this happens, it is never party/fun for the butler. It is always about staying professional because the butler should always be mindful that in the morning, he/she still has these same guests to take care of, so at the party, you are still at work.

CAN A BUTLER BUY LOCAL COOK FOOD OUTSIDE OF THE RESORT FOR A GUEST?

No!

This topic is a very delicate one. We do have cases where guests request the butler to buy food outside the resort. In most cases, the guest hears about a restaurant by word of mouth or by reading up about it online. The reviews might be very good, but the resort cannot verify if that local food outlet stores their food properly. Therefore, this practice is prohibited by the hotel/villa.

If the guest is very persistent about this matter, there are two ways the hotel can play this off. One way is to have the guests sign a waiver document to say that the hotel is not responsible in case they become ill, or the hotel can inform the guests that the resort does not promote this practice, so if they proceed, they do so at their own risk. However, we do have cases where guests go out to eat. What we do in these cases is to refer them to a taxi on the resort, and they can pursue on their own discretion.

There have been cases where guests check-in for an entire week and have not consumed any meal from the hotel where they are staying. They travel with their own meals for every day; usually these people are vegetarians, have high allergic reactions, or have decided to play it safe when traveling.

There is another set of guests who are known as kosher guest. Their religion does not allow them to eat from any pots that meat has been cooked in before. It doesn't mean that they don't eat meat, but the pot must be new pots, and the meat has to be killed and prepared a particular way that is often a long process. So, what they do is take their own meals wherever they are going, or they try their best to ensure that the resort they are staying has a restaurant on property. If not, there is a kosher outlet nearby that can supply meals while they are there.

CAN A BUTLER ASK A GUEST FOR MONEY?

This practice is a NO NO!

Most organizations in the hospitality industry and other company policies prohibit soliciting tips from the customer/s. Once an offense such as this is carried out by any member of staff, it warrants immediate investigation, and if proven, it will result in dismissal according to several policies. The same applies to the butler; this offense will result in him/her losing their job. Please note that tipping a butler is a gesture by the guest. They may or may not decide to tip their butler based on the type of service they receive from their butler, whether it is good or bad.

There are cases where butlers deliver exceptional service throughout the duration of the guest's stay, and the guests leave and tell the butler "Thank you." Even in these cases, the butler doesn't have the right to ask for ANY MONEY from the guest.

In the hotel industry, this is considered a termination offense.

CAN MY BUTLER BABYSIT MY CHILD/CHILDREN WHILE I GO FOR DINNER?

Yes, depending on the policy of the hotel. Most hotels that cater to families normally carry a kid's camp service or babysitting service that includes services such as babysitting and night care services, which normally come at an additional charge per child per hour. In some cases, a guest may request their butler to babysit their child/children depending on the level of trust they have for the butler around their kids. These guests would have to seek permission from the hotel management for the butler to proceed with this service. Please take into consideration that the butler will have other guests that they will need to attend to. Babysitting a child or two will require the butler's full attention to the child, and he may have to proceed with service after their shift. You may have to pay additional money for your own personal butler, which means the butler will only be assigned to your family given the fact that butlers take care of more than one room or more than one family. Please note that this service is based on the butler's disquisition; it's not mandatory.

HAVE YOU EVER WALKED INTO ANY GUEST ROOM WHILE THEY ARE HAVING SEX?

Wow, and yes!

As a butler, we are trained to maintain our composure in situations like these. I have had cases where guests requested for me to take drinks and food to their room. Upon entering the room, I would have called to advise them that I was on my way to the room with their request. Upon knocking at the door, they replied that I should enter. Now while walking in, I realized what was taking place, so I apologized. They said it was no problem, and I should enter. I placed their request in the room, and they proceeded with what they were doing. This action happens over and over and with several different guests and butlers. Like I always say: Once the guest gets to know you and feels comfortable around you, as their butler, expect anything from them. I won't mention too much on this topic as I am writing another book on this topic and experience.

HAVE I EVER BEEN IN A POSITION WHERE I AM ACCUSED OF THEFT, AND HOW DID I DEAL WITH IT?

Oh, yes. Honesty is always the best policy. It is always okay for guests to accuse you. However, once you know that you are not guilty, there should not be any reason for you to worry or panic. There is a series or level of investigation that the butler must undergo. In some cases, you are removed from the shift until a verdict is reached. The investigation may be intense based on the results of the investigation. Once you are proven not guilty, you will return to your duties.

Once proven guilty, the butler immediately loses his/her job along with anyone else who is involved. You do have cases where the butler is not guilty, and he/she still loses their job. Some resorts fail to complete the process or channel for investigation. What they do is just give the guests right and proceed with disciplinary action against the staff. Sometimes the resorts value the customer's comments or feedback, especially if they are repeaters to the brand. Most resorts believe in the tag line that says, "THE GUEST IS ALWAYS RIGHT," so they will act on a simple complaint from the customer.

HAVE YOU EVER BEEN DISRESPECTED BY A GUEST AND HOW DID YOU DEAL WITH IT?

Yes, countless times. One of the key factors of being a very good butler is tolerance, patience, and humility. 90% of guests who pass through your hand as a butler will test one of these areas, but being a butler, you have to bite your tongue, hold your peace and let the professional side of you overcome your personal feelings.

In an industry like hospitality, there are a lot of things that both guests and staff members will do or say that will cause your emotional feelings to stand up. We are human beings and do have feelings and are eager; however, there is a phrase that I always remind myself ever so often, and that is "Not to take things too personal." At all times, try to be professional and diplomatic.

We have cases where a guest will disrespect you on arrival and still expect the best service from you. Being a service professional, the aim is, at all times, to deliver the best service we can. We should not look for an apology.

I had a case where a guest told my partner that "He should blow cold air up his ass and wait for it to come back as hot air." What made it worse, he was trying to encourage the butler, claiming that he was giving him a motivational speech. The guest found it so funny, while my partner was not even smiling about it.

An example of some disrespect a butler faces daily are as follow:

- Slamming the door in the butler's face because something the hotel provided was not in their package.
- Call you their bitch or other racist names.
- Tell your boss you have never done anything for them, knowing it is a lie, just to get something free.
- Using a lot of expletives towards you.
- Show racism towards you (as if you are a slave).
- Leave dirty underwear and used condoms on the floor and expect you to pick them up and clean up after them or their room.

This list could go on and on.

HAVE YOU EVER BEEN IN A POSITION WHERE A GUEST TOUCHED YOU INAPPROPRIATELY, AND HOW DID YOU DEAL WITH IT?

Yes, I have been in a position where women have touched me inappropriately in a room by hitting me on my butt. I dealt with it in a way where I don't let the guest feel small, but body language says a lot, and once they realize that you are not into what they are up to, they always stand down.

One thing we must remember is that tourists come on vacation for many different reasons. See below for a list of a few reasons:

- To find a husband or wife.
- To get married.
- To celebrate their birthday, honeymoon, anniversary, baby shower, etc.
- To relax and have clean fun.
- To try our drugs (weed).
- To have sex with another male or female in another country.
- To commit suicide.
- As their last death wish.
- Because it is on their bucket list.

HAVE YOU EVER HAD TO UNDRESS A GUEST, AND HOW DID YOU DEAL WITH IT?

Yes, I cannot forget taking care of a travel agent in my early days of becoming a butler. Now this travel agent was one of the top agents for a top company that I used to work for. She called for me to escort her to her room. The moment we left the lobby for the room, I realized she was a bit intoxicated. Upon gaining entrance to her room, she started to undress herself and went straight into her bathroom. I attempted to leave, and she insisted that I didn't leave. I held my peace and, most of all, my composure.

While she was in the bathroom, she asked me to assist her with unpacking. While unpacking, I heard the bathroom door open. I thought she was in her robe, but to my surprise, this lady was naked in front of me. She walked toward me and said she had to find something to wear later for a travel agent cocktail party. She asked what I thought she should wear. I picked out a dress. She then said she needed an underwear, so I picked out a matching one for her dress. She then got dressed and left for the function. That experience lasted for six days out of her vacation. I went directly to the general manager's office and informed him of the situation because the guest could go to the lobby and say I tried to rape her or even that I was stalking her. The rest of this information will be in my other book with more details.

WHAT'S THE LARGEST TIP A BUTLER EVER RECEIVED FROM A GUEST?

Wow!

The largest tip! Please be reminded that tips come in two forms: cash and non-cash, such as items and jesters. I remember when I was getting married, I was blessed to have a guest pay for a yacht for me and my wife to sail around for a day. I have had guests who tipped me over US$1,000, and the list goes on. One thing I have come to realize in this industry of being a butler is, your largest tip doesn't come from the rich; it comes from someone who really appreciates your service and values what you do for them. These customers take the time out to see that the butler is going above and beyond the call of duty to ensure they are having the best time of their life.

Let me say this, sometimes the biggest tip is a genuine thank you that comes from their heart. It is better than money in this line of work.

We have cases where the guests help complete the butler's unfinished house; we have cases where guests pay for the butler to go back to university that cost thousands of USD, and there are cases where the butler has a close loved one pass off, and the guests pay for the entire funeral arrangement. Let me say this, at no point did the butler ask (solicit) a tip from the guests, but these are cases where the butler did such a wonderful job, and the guests accepted the butler as family.

HAVE YOU EVER BEEN IN THE MIDDLE OF A COUPLE WHO IS FIGHTING, AND HOW DID YOU DEAL WITH IT?

Yes.

Can I tell you, it is one of the most embarrassing moments for a butler to walk into. Why? Because they often want us to take a side to prove that one of the other parties involved is wrong. The best way to deal with this is always trying to stay out of it. If you can't stay out, stay neutral with your response; allow them to work it out on their own.

Most times these fights start because of too much drinking of alcoholic beverages or because one of the parties feels insecure about something that the other party did, but one thing is for sure, before the day is out, they will make it up to each other. So, because of that, as butlers, we always stay away from it, or we refuse to even give any response to this type of situation.

WHICH COUNTRY/ISLAND OR NATIONALITY OF GUESTS DOES THE BUTLER FIND TO BE MOST DISRESPECTFUL?

Wow!

This is a very hard question but, to be honest, I find that Indian and Russian guests are very rude and disrespectful. You will find some nice ones, but a majority of them that I have served and having done surveys with other butlers, we have proven that Indians are the most disrespectful guest to deal with.

Let me share a story that took place at work with me and one of my partners. We were talking with one of our guests, who happens to be an Indian. He was giving my partner a motivational speech about staying focused. He started off by saying, "People are going to give you a hard time but don't give up." Listen, his words were, and I quote, "Sometimes you have to blow cold air up a guest's asshole and sit there by the guest's asshole and wait for it to come back down to you as hot air." I do understand what he was trying to say, but I think he was just being rude. My partner at the time didn't leave feeling motivated but rather disrespected. I saw where he was rather disturbed by the comment because he spoke about it for weeks thereafter.

WHICH COUNTRY DOES A BUTLER FIND TO BE MORE RACIST?

Wow!

After doing a survey, along with working in the position for over a decade, I have come to realize that the Indians hold the number one spot, followed by the Americans. Again, let me clear the air by saying not all Indians and Americans are like that, but they will complain even if there is nothing to complain about. The Indians are always trying to prove a point to say that they are the biggest wherever they go, and they don't want to pay for a certain level of service but require the best of everything without paying, even if there is no cost. When you try to explain, they look down and talk to you as if you are a nobody. They want you to just make it happen. Again, not all Indians are like this. I have personally dealt with some nice ones, but the majority rules. This does not get the best of us as butlers as we are trained as professionals. We always find a way to get around this behavior and still deliver a professional service.

WHAT IS THE WEIRDEST THING A GUEST HAS EVER ASKED A BUTLER FOR?

Wow!

I have had a lot of weird requests. However, this one stood out the most. I remember being at work, and a guest called asking me where they could find the closest sex shop/adult toy store to the resort? He wanted me to purchase a dildo for his wife because she left hers at home. He went on to tell me the size that she wanted, the color, shape, and length. He also wanted me to buy some sex pills to help improve his bedroom problem and find lingerie for his wife to wear. Now as a butler, we find this to be fun. What we do is, we don't let the guests feel small or less of a man or woman. We assure them that we will get it done and whatever we do, we keep it confidential and maintain a high level of professionalism as a butler. On arrival, we often assure the guest that no question is too crazy for the butler. This lets them feel comfortable asking for every and anything.

In most cases, we have to reassure them, once it is legal and ethical.

HAVE YOU EVER TRAVELED BEFORE AND WHERE HAVE YOU BEEN?

Guest will often ask you this question to start a conversation. Most times they want to know because some people view Jamaica as a third-world country, and we may or may not have traveled anywhere outside of the island given the restrictions imposed on us to enter other countries. This question can also be considered as a medium for getting to familiarize themselves with you as their butler better, and not just as their butler, but to understand who you are as a person. I have come to the realization that this question tells the guest that you are exposed to different cultures, and it makes you, as a butler, be able to relate to them on an international level. In today's world, we have books that we can read that will take you all over the world. Most of all, the world is just one click or scroll away on the internet. As we always say, "Information is power."

WHERE DO BUTLERS GO FOR VACATION?

Pampering is the number one service that butlers provide to his/her guest daily. For the butler, as it relates to vacation, they will travel outside of their country of work to relax and experience something different, especially the ones who have a visa. For the ones who may not hold a visa, they tend to use the time to visit friends and family within the island or complete an excursion that they might have wanted to do for a while. For some, they will use the time to get some rest as they know the busy season is drawing close. This is also the time that butlers often use to get new items to improve their work environment, such as items they use to wow and surprise their guests but, most of all, they use the time to bond with their significant other, for those who have one.

DOES YOUR LEADER TREAT YOU WELL AS A BUTLER IN THIS COMPANY THAT YOU ARE WORKING FOR?

This is another question that is asked by many guests. For me, my response is always "Yes." A butler's position in the hotel is considered to be a very high position, one that is treated with respect and high standard. One of the many reasons is because the butlers are the ones who are trained to take care of all VIP guests; the rich and famous, and the top priority clients who walk in and out of the hotel. The standard of a butler is always expected to be maintained on a high level, and they are always expected to be service professionals, hence we are treated very well and with a lot of respect.

WHAT IS THE FREAKIEST THING A GUEST EVER ASKED A BUTLER FOR?

On a day-to-day basis, we interact with many different guests of different beliefs and cultures. I remember taking care of a couple, and the husband requested for a male butler to have sexual intercourse with his wife while he sat back and enjoyed the show. When the butler declined, the husband wanted to know how much it would cost for someone to fulfill his request. On the other hand, I have seen and heard of female guests who have asked their butlers to participate in a threesome intercourse with them and their partners or even two female friends with a Jamaican guy. Oh, yes! This has happened, and they do get what they ask for sometimes.

I won't say much on this topic as it will be in my next book.

WHAT IS THE FREAKIEST THING A GUEST EVER ASKED YOU TO DO?

We expect anything from our guests as they have different cultures and beliefs and because clients travel for many different reasons. One of the freakiest requests a guest has ever asked me for is to video him and his wife while they were having sex. Just to add to this request, the butler has all right to decline. Did I video the guests having sex? There is only one way to find out. Get a copy of my next book where I will share my experience much deeper and reveal some of the secrets of the butler service.

Another guest I was butlering called me to come to the room. Upon arrival, she was naked. She then asked me to pick out items for her to wear daily and nightly. For one week, we talked about her attire, from underwear to dress, and while I looked for the items for her to wear, she was not in a robe or towel covering up; she was naked walking around the room. Did she try to make a move on me? If yes, what did I do? Look out for the answer in my next book.

WOULD YOU DO BUTLER SERVICE OUTSIDE OF JAMAICA?

This is a two-way answer. For me, it is a yes and no answer.

Yes, for the experience of taking on the challenge of working in a new environment and dealing with a new culture as well as being able to share my knowledge, but this depends on where and what are the terms and conditions.

As a Jamaican butler, our butler service is a bit of a twist compared to other places in the world. One thing for sure is that the basic butler service doesn't change no matter what twist you want to add to it. Most hotels are now expecting more out of their butlers, and at the same time they are limiting the tools for them to work with, resulting in the butlers going outside of the box to make it happen for the guests, which often leads to overworking the butler to get the job done. So, as I always say, it all depends on the job condition and the tools that we are given to work with.

About the Author

Kenton A. Grayson has been in the hospitality industry for over eleven years. He started out at Beaches Boscobel Hotel and then went to work at Sandals Royal Bahamian for a short period in the Bahamas.

He started his butler journey at Sandals Royal Plantation Resort, then moved on to the Bahia Principe Resort, and is now currently working at the Hyatt Ziva and Zilara Resort in St. James. He entered the hotel industry as an air condition and refrigeration technician in the engineering department; of the seventeen years, he has over twelve years of experience in butler service.

He is trained by the Guild of English Professional Butlers by Robert Watson, where he graduated with distinction while working with Sandals Resort

International Company. He later moved on to work for other companies. He underwent training where he was certified by Exceeding Expectation Limited E.E. by Robin Stewart, who is endorsed by the Institute of Hospitality in England.

Kenton A. Grayson has developed a strong love for butler service along with an eye for details. Throughout the years, he has been privileged to talk with prime ministers from all over the Caribbean, as well as billionaires from all over the world such as Sheik, war veterans, and the list goes on.

Come and join him on his butler journey as his story and tales never end.

Made in the USA
Columbia, SC
17 February 2025

54012681R00037